6 Sigma Yellow Belt

Building Your Foundation for Leading and
Supporting Process Improvement Projects

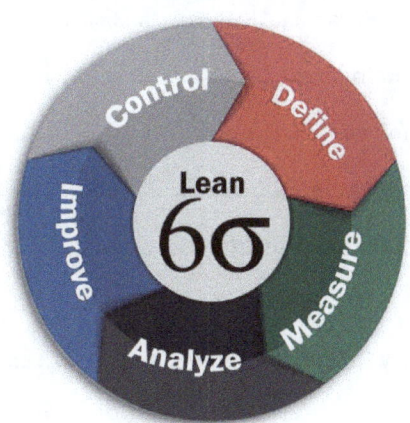

Contents

6 Sigma Yellow Belt Course Outline

Course Objectives

1. Gain a deeper understanding of Six Sigma principles and the DMAIC methodology.
2. Learn about additional Six Sigma tools and how to apply them effectively in small projects.
3. Develop the skills needed to lead small-scale Six Sigma projects within your department.
4. Understand the Yellow Belt's role in supporting Green and Black Belts.
5. Gain practical experience through exercises and case studies.

Module 1: Six Sigma Refresher

Objective: Review the core principles from White Belt training to ensure participants have a solid understanding of Six Sigma basics before moving to more advanced topics.

Key Concepts to Review:

- Six Sigma Goals: Aim to reduce defects and variation to meet customer expectations consistently.
- DMAIC Phases: Define, Measure, Analyse, Improve, Control.
- Key Six Sigma Tools: Check Sheets, Histograms, Control Charts, Pareto Charts, Process Flow Diagrams.

1

- Six Sigma Culture: Emphasise quality, continuous improvement, and data-driven decisions.

Activity: Have participants summarise the DMAIC process in their own words and discuss how they have used White Belt tools in their work since their initial training.

Module 2: Yellow Belt Responsibilities

Objective: Help participants understand the unique role of a Yellow Belt, including responsibilities and expectations.

Yellow Belt Key Responsibilities:

1. Leading Small Projects: Yellow Belts can take on small, department-focused projects, following the DMAIC process to improve specific areas.
2. Supporting Higher-Level Belts: They play a key role in gathering data, assisting with problem-solving, and implementing solutions for larger Six Sigma projects.
3. Applying Six Sigma Tools: Yellow Belts use more advanced tools than White Belts and develop expertise in data collection and analysis.
4. Training and Mentoring White Belts: Yellow Belts often provide support and guidance to White Belts within their teams.

Example: A Yellow Belt in customer service might lead a project to reduce average response times by identifying bottlenecks and implementing small process improvements.

Activity: Ask participants to discuss a process in their area that could benefit from a Yellow Belt-led improvement project.

Module 3: Deeper Dive into DMAIC

This module provides a detailed breakdown of each DMAIC phase, with specific activities and tools that Yellow Belts will use to lead small projects.

Define Phase
Objective: Clearly identify the problem, establish goals, and determine the project's scope.

Key Activities:

- Develop a Project Charter: Outline the problem, goals, scope, timeline, and team members involved.
- Voice of the Customer (VoC): Gather customer insights to identify what's critical to quality (CTQ).
- Stakeholder Identification: Identify who will benefit from or be impacted by the project.

Example Tool: SIPOC Diagram, which provides a high-level map of Suppliers, Inputs, Process, Outputs, and Customers.

Activity: Have participants create a SIPOC diagram for a process they work with regularly.

Measure Phase
Objective: Gather data to understand the current process and establish a baseline for improvement.

Key Activities:

- Define Key Metrics: Identify metrics that align with project goals, such as defect rate or cycle time.
- Data Collection Plan: Create a structured plan outlining what data to collect, how, and when.
- Measurement System Analysis (MSA): Ensure that measurement tools and methods are reliable.

Example Tool: Gage Repeatability and Reproducibility (Gage R&R) for verifying measurement consistency.

Activity: Have participants outline a simple data collection plan for their chosen project area.

Analyse Phase
Objective: Identify root causes of the problem using data analysis and root cause analysis tools.

Key Activities:

- Process Mapping: Use detailed process maps to identify inefficiencies and bottlenecks.
- Root Cause Analysis: Use tools like the 5 Whys and Fishbone Diagram to drill down to the root causes.
- Data Analysis: Perform basic data analysis to identify patterns or trends contributing to the problem.

Example Tool: Fishbone Diagram to categorise possible causes.

Activity: Ask participants to choose a recurring issue in their area and use a Fishbone Diagram to explore potential root causes.

Improve Phase

Objective: Develop, implement, and test solutions to address the root causes identified.

Key Activities:

- Solution Brainstorming: Generate a list of potential solutions and evaluate their feasibility and impact.
- Pilot Testing: Test selected solutions on a small scale before full implementation.
- Implementation Plan: Create a clear plan for rolling out the solution, including necessary training and resources.

Example Tool: Solution Prioritisation Matrix to assess which solutions offer the best balance of impact and feasibility.

Activity: Have participants outline a pilot test plan for a solution to their chosen problem.

Control Phase

Objective: Ensure that the improvements are sustained over time.

Key Activities:

- Develop Control Plans: Define how the process will be monitored and maintained.
- Standard Operating Procedures (SOPs): Document the improved process and create SOPs if needed.
- Monitoring and Reporting: Set up regular checks and reporting to ensure continued process stability.

Example Tool: Control Chart to monitor performance over time and detect any deviations.

Activity: Ask participants to create a simple control plan for maintaining improvements in their project area.

Module 4: Advanced Six Sigma Tools for Yellow Belts

This module introduces new tools that Yellow Belts will use to support their analysis and improvement efforts.

1. Cause-and-Effect Matrix

- Purpose: Helps prioritise potential causes of a problem based on their impact on CTQs.
- Activity: Have participants use a sample Cause-and-Effect Matrix to rank factors affecting a process.

2. Failure Modes and Effects Analysis (FMEA)

- Purpose: Assesses potential failures in a process and ranks them based on risk.
- Activity: Provide a simple FMEA template and guide participants through completing one for a process they're familiar with.

3. Process Capability Analysis

- Purpose: Determines whether a process can consistently meet customer specifications.
- Activity: Ask participants to calculate basic capability indices (e.g., Cp and Cpk) for a process with sample data.

Module 5: Leading a Small Six Sigma Project

This module focuses on guiding Yellow Belts through the practical aspects of leading a small Six Sigma project, from selecting a project to implementing solutions.

Steps to Leading a Yellow Belt Project:

1. Identify a Suitable Project: Look for small, manageable projects with clear goals and a limited scope.
2. Define the Team: Assemble a small team and clarify roles and responsibilities.
3. Set Clear Objectives: Establish specific, measurable goals aligned with the business's CTQs.
4. Use DMAIC for Project Management: Follow the DMAIC process to ensure a structured approach to problem-solving.

Example Project: Reducing cycle time in an administrative process by identifying bottlenecks and implementing process changes.

Activity: Have participants outline a plan for a small Six Sigma project in their work area, including goals, timeline, and team roles.

Module 6: Supporting Green and Black Belts

Objective: Help Yellow Belts understand how to assist higher-level belts with data collection, analysis, and implementation support.

Ways Yellow Belts Support Higher Belts:

- Data Collection and Reporting: Gathering and summarising data for analysis by Green or Black Belts.
- Implementation Assistance: Assisting with piloting or rolling out solutions in their department.
- Observational Feedback: Reporting on the effectiveness of changes and providing feedback for further improvement.

Activity: Ask participants to share examples of how they could support a Green or Black Belt project in their work area.

Module 7: Encouraging a Continuous Improvement Culture

Objective: Reinforce the importance of fostering a culture of quality and improvement within the team.

Key Practices:

1. Promote Data-Driven Thinking: Encourage colleagues to make decisions based on facts and data.
2. Encourage Small Improvements: Foster a mindset where every team member is looking for ways to improve their tasks.
3. Celebrate Wins: Recognise and celebrate even small improvements, reinforcing the value of continuous improvement.

Activity: Ask participants to set a personal goal for promoting Six Sigma principles within their team, such as encouraging colleagues to use data or suggesting a small improvement.

Module 8: Summary and Next Steps

This module wraps up the course, summarising key takeaways and encouraging participants to continue learning and apply their skills.

Recap of Yellow Belt Skills:

- Understanding DMAIC in greater depth and using advanced Six Sigma tools.
- Leading small projects and supporting higher-level belts.
- Promoting a culture of continuous improvement within the team.

Pathways for Further Learning:

- Green Belt Certification: Moving to Green Belt for more advanced projects and leadership roles.
- Six Sigma Resources: Books, online courses, and mentorship opportunities for ongoing learning.

Final Activity: Encourage participants to create a personal action plan for applying Yellow Belt skills in their role,

Module 1: Six Sigma Refresher

Course Objective for Module 1

By the end of this module, participants should have a strong grasp of Six Sigma fundamentals, including its purpose, key principles, and the DMAIC methodology. This module ensures that everyone starts with a solid understanding of Six Sigma basics before moving into the more advanced topics covered in the Yellow Belt course.

---

1. What is Six Sigma? – A Quick Recap

Definition of Six Sigma:
Six Sigma is a data-driven methodology designed to improve processes by identifying and reducing defects and variations. The ultimate goal is to meet or exceed customer expectations by creating more consistent and reliable processes.

The Origins of Six Sigma:

- Developed at Motorola in the 1980s, Six Sigma initially aimed to improve product quality in manufacturing.
- It has since been adopted across many industries, including healthcare, finance, and services, as a general framework for improving quality and efficiency.

The Meaning of "Six Sigma":

- In statistical terms, "Six Sigma" refers to achieving a level of quality where only 3.4 defects occur per million opportunities (DPMO).
- This level represents near-perfection, where processes are highly controlled and variations are minimal.

Example of Six Sigma Application:
Consider an online retail company aiming to reduce packaging errors. By applying Six Sigma, they could systematically identify where errors occur, analyse causes, and implement changes to ensure orders are accurately packed.

Activity:
Ask participants to think of a process in their area where consistency and quality are crucial. Have them share how achieving a "Six Sigma level" of quality could benefit that process.

---

2. Key Principles of Six Sigma

This section reviews the foundational principles that drive Six Sigma projects and culture.

Principle 1: Customer Focus

- The core of Six Sigma is understanding and meeting customer needs.
- Projects should always start by identifying what's most important to the customer, often referred to as "Critical to Quality" (CTQ) elements.

Principle 2: Data-Driven Decision Making

- Six Sigma relies on collecting and analysing data to make informed decisions, rather than relying on assumptions or opinions.
- This data-driven approach ensures that improvements are based on facts and evidence.

Principle 3: Continuous Improvement

- Six Sigma promotes a mindset of continuous improvement, meaning processes should always be re-evaluated and improved.
- Even if a process is stable, Six Sigma encourages seeking ways to enhance quality, reduce waste, or improve efficiency.

Principle 4: Process and Variation Control

- Six Sigma focuses on reducing variation within a process, which leads to more consistent and reliable outcomes.
- By controlling variation, Six Sigma projects minimise the likelihood of defects or errors.

Activity:
Ask participants to pick one of these principles and think of how it could apply to their current role. Have them share examples of how focusing on the customer, data, or continuous improvement has helped in past projects or tasks.

---

3. Overview of the DMAIC Process

The DMAIC process is the core methodology of Six Sigma. As Yellow Belts, participants will be expected to lead small projects using DMAIC, so it's essential that they understand each phase in depth.

Quick Review of Each Phase:

1. Define: Identify the problem, set clear objectives, and understand the customer's requirements.
2. Measure: Collect data to understand the current state of the process and establish a baseline.
3. Analyse: Use data to identify the root causes of the problem.
4. Improve: Develop and implement solutions to address the root causes.
5. Control: Put systems in place to ensure the improvements are sustained over time.

Example of DMAIC in Action:
Consider a Yellow Belt-led project to reduce waiting times at a hospital reception. Using DMAIC, they would:

1. Define the issue of long wait times and set a goal for reduction.
2. Measure current waiting times to establish a baseline.
3. Analyse the process to identify bottlenecks causing delays.
4. Implement changes, such as reorganising staff schedules, to reduce bottlenecks.
5. Monitor the wait times over time to ensure the improvement is maintained.

Activity:
Have participants choose a minor process they're familiar with

and outline how they would apply each DMAIC phase to improve it.

---

4. Key Six Sigma Tools Recap

Yellow Belts will be using a range of Six Sigma tools, both basic and advanced, to manage their projects. Here's a quick refresher on some essential tools introduced in White Belt training.

1. Check Sheets

- Purpose: Collect data in a simple, structured way.
- Application: Useful for tracking how often certain issues occur.
- Example: Recording the number of customer complaints each day.

2. Histograms

- Purpose: Show the distribution of data, helping teams understand variation.
- Application: Useful for seeing if most data points cluster around a certain value.
- Example: Tracking delivery times to see if most fall within an acceptable range.

3. Control Charts

- Purpose: Monitor process stability over time by tracking data points and spotting deviations.

- Application: Helps identify if a process is stable or if there are unusual variations.
- Example: Tracking daily production output to ensure it stays within control limits.

4. Pareto Charts

- Purpose: Identify the "vital few" causes of issues, based on the 80/20 rule.
- Application: Useful for focusing improvement efforts on the most significant problems.
- Example: Analysing customer complaints by type to see which issues are most frequent.

5. Process Flow Diagrams

- Purpose: Map out the steps in a process, providing a visual representation.
- Application: Useful for identifying unnecessary steps, bottlenecks, or redundancies.
- Example: Mapping the steps in the customer returns process to find areas to streamline.

Activity:
Ask participants to choose one of these tools and describe a specific process in their work where they could apply it. Discuss how this tool could help them gain insights into the process and identify improvement opportunities.

---

5. Six Sigma Culture Refresher

Key Elements of a Six Sigma Culture:

1. Focus on Quality: Every team member is responsible for maintaining and improving quality in their work.
2. Data and Facts Matter: Decisions are based on data, not assumptions or guesses.
3. Continuous Improvement Mindset: Employees are encouraged to always look for ways to improve processes, even in small ways.
4. Team Collaboration: Six Sigma relies on teamwork, with people from different areas collaborating to achieve common goals.

How Yellow Belts Contribute to Six Sigma Culture:

- Actively Participate in Improvement Projects: Yellow Belts lead small projects and provide support on larger projects.
- Encourage Data-Driven Decisions: By collecting data and using Six Sigma tools, Yellow Belts help their teams rely on facts to make improvements.
- Promote a Positive, Solution-Focused Attitude: Yellow Belts help foster a mindset of continuous improvement within their departments.

Activity:
Ask participants to think about how they can promote a Six Sigma culture in their role, whether by encouraging data collection, suggesting improvements, or collaborating with their team.

---

6. Setting Goals for Yellow Belt Training

Objective: Help participants identify what they hope to achieve from Yellow Belt training, so they can apply the knowledge effectively in their role.

Steps to Set Personal Goals:

1. Reflect on Areas for Improvement: Identify processes in their work that could benefit from improvement.
2. Set Clear, Measurable Goals: Define what they want to achieve with their Yellow Belt knowledge (e.g., reduce waste, improve efficiency).
3. Think of Practical Applications: Consider specific tasks where they can apply DMAIC and Six Sigma tools.

Example Goals:

- A participant in inventory management might set a goal to reduce stockouts by 15%.
- A participant in customer service could aim to improve first-call resolution rates by implementing data-based process improvements.

Activity:
Have participants write down one or two goals they'd like to achieve through this training, along with ideas for how they'll measure success. This goal-setting exercise will help them approach the course with a practical, action-oriented mindset.

Key Takeaways from Module 1

1. Six Sigma is a data-driven approach focused on reducing defects and meeting customer expectations.

2. DMAIC is the core methodology, providing a structured, step-by-step approach to solving problems and improving processes.
3. Key Six Sigma tools like Check Sheets, Histograms, and Pareto Charts help Yellow Belts analyse data and identify improvement opportunities.
4. A Six Sigma culture prioritises quality, data, continuous improvement, and collaboration, and Yellow Belts play an essential role in promoting these values within their teams.

Final Activity for Module 1: Reflection Exercise

Objective: Have participants reflect on what they've reviewed in this module and identify key concepts they feel most comfortable with, as well as any areas they'd like to explore further.

Instructions:

1. Ask participants to reflect on which areas they feel confident about and which they need to review.
2. Invite them to share any specific areas they're excited to apply in their work or any questions they still have.

Outcome: This exercise encourages participants to take ownership of their learning and reinforces the idea that Yellow Belts are active contributors to Six Sigma projects and culture.

Module 2: Yellow Belt Responsibilities

Course Objective for Module 2

By the end of this module, participants should understand the responsibilities of a Yellow Belt in Six Sigma projects, including leading small improvement projects, supporting higher-level belts, and promoting Six Sigma principles in their work areas.

---

1. The Role of a Yellow Belt in Six Sigma

Overview of Yellow Belt Responsibilities: Yellow Belts are the bridge between White Belts (who focus on observing and supporting) and Green/Black Belts (who lead large projects). Yellow Belts play a hands-on role in implementing improvements, particularly within their own departments or teams. They:

- Lead Small Projects: Use DMAIC to address specific issues in their area.
- Support Green and Black Belts: Assist in data collection, analysis, and implementation on larger projects.
- Promote Six Sigma Culture: Encourage continuous improvement, data-driven thinking, and teamwork within their teams.

Example of Yellow Belt Responsibilities: A Yellow Belt in customer service might lead a project to reduce the average call handling time, while supporting a Green Belt-led project to improve overall customer satisfaction metrics.

Activity:
Ask participants to identify a small project in their area that they could lead or support, focusing on a specific problem or improvement opportunity.

2. Leading Small Projects with DMAIC

Yellow Belt Leadership in Small Projects:
Yellow Belts have the skills to lead small-scale projects independently, using DMAIC to guide the improvement process. These projects are typically focused on one area or team, and Yellow Belts are responsible for planning, implementing, and sustaining improvements.

Steps for Leading a Small Project:

1. Define the Problem: Identify a clear, specific issue and determine the project's goals.
2. Measure Current Performance: Collect baseline data to understand the current state.
3. Analyse Root Causes: Use data and Six Sigma tools to identify the main causes of the problem.
4. Implement Improvements: Develop, test, and implement solutions.
5. Control and Sustain: Put measures in place to ensure improvements are maintained.

Example Project: In a warehouse, a Yellow Belt might lead a project to reduce the frequency of misplaced items. Using DMAIC, they would define the issue, collect data on item locations, analyse causes (e.g., labelling errors or staff training gaps), implement changes, and monitor to sustain improvements.

Activity:
Ask participants to outline a small project idea, including the problem they would address and a basic DMAIC plan for each phase.

---

3. Supporting Higher-Level Belts

Role of Yellow Belts in Larger Projects:
Yellow Belts support Green and Black Belts on larger, cross-functional projects. They help with tasks like data collection, process observation, and initial analysis, and they assist with implementing changes in their department.

Examples of Support Tasks:

- Data Collection and Reporting: Yellow Belts gather and organise data from their area, providing valuable information for Green and Black Belt analysis.
- Initial Process Mapping: Yellow Belts can create or update process flow diagrams, highlighting any observed issues or bottlenecks.
- Implementation Assistance: They help implement changes, conduct pilot tests, and ensure team members understand and follow new procedures.

Example of Support Role: In a finance department project to reduce invoice processing time, a Yellow Belt might collect data on current processing times and document the steps of the process. They could also support the team in rolling out new digital tools or revised workflows.

Activity:
Ask participants to think of a large project in their workplace where they could assist a Green or Black Belt. Have them identify specific tasks they could take on to support the project.

---

4. Key Skills for Yellow Belts

Yellow Belts need specific skills to effectively lead small projects and support larger initiatives. This module covers essential skills that will help them contribute meaningfully to Six Sigma projects.

Skill 1: Project Management Basics
Yellow Belts need basic project management skills to organise their work, set timelines, assign tasks, and track progress. Simple project management tools, such as timelines and checklists, are useful for keeping small projects on track.

Skill 2: Data Collection and Analysis
Accurate data collection is essential for identifying root causes and measuring improvements. Yellow Belts should be able to set up a data collection plan, use check sheets, and perform basic data analysis.

Skill 3: Root Cause Analysis
Root cause analysis helps Yellow Belts identify the real reasons behind a problem, rather than just addressing symptoms. Tools

like the 5 Whys and Fishbone Diagrams allow them to dig deeper into process issues.

Skill 4: Communication and Collaboration
Yellow Belts need strong communication skills to work with team members, explain project goals, and provide updates to higher-level belts. Collaboration is also crucial, as they often work with people from other departments.

Activity:
Have participants choose one of these skills and discuss how they could apply it in a current project or task. This helps them think about practical applications of their Yellow Belt skills.

---

5. Leading and Facilitating Team Meetings

Yellow Belts are often responsible for leading team meetings related to their projects, especially when discussing issues, sharing updates, or reviewing progress.

Tips for Leading Effective Meetings:

1. Set a Clear Agenda: Outline what topics will be covered and stick to the agenda.
2. Encourage Participation: Create an open environment where team members feel comfortable sharing ideas.
3. Focus on Solutions: Keep discussions focused on finding solutions rather than just highlighting problems.
4. Summarise Key Points and Next Steps: Recap the discussion and make sure everyone knows their tasks and responsibilities.

Example:
A Yellow Belt leading a project to improve order accuracy in a retail store might hold a weekly meeting with team members to review progress, discuss challenges, and share updates on improvement efforts.

Activity:
Ask participants to outline a brief agenda for a team meeting about a small project in their area. This practice reinforces the importance of structured communication.

---

6. Promoting Six Sigma Culture within Teams

Role of Yellow Belts in Fostering Six Sigma Culture:
Yellow Belts are advocates of Six Sigma culture, helping reinforce a mindset of quality, efficiency, and continuous improvement. They act as role models for data-driven decision-making and collaboration.

Ways Yellow Belts Can Promote Six Sigma Culture:

- Encourage Data Use: Promote the use of data to make decisions and solve problems.
- Celebrate Small Wins: Recognise and celebrate even small improvements to build morale and encourage ongoing improvements.
- Provide Mentorship to White Belts: Guide White Belts in understanding Six Sigma basics, answering questions, and helping them see how they can contribute.
- Highlight Customer Focus: Emphasise that improvements should always aim to enhance customer

satisfaction, whether internal (employees) or external (customers).

Example:
In a manufacturing plant, a Yellow Belt might encourage their team to track defects more closely and suggest small changes to improve quality, such as checking materials more frequently or standardising workflows.

Activity:
Ask participants to think of one way they could promote Six Sigma principles within their team, whether through data, recognition, or mentorship. Discuss how these actions contribute to a positive work culture.

---

7. Tracking and Reporting Progress

Importance of Tracking Progress:
Effective tracking and reporting are essential to measure the impact of improvements and demonstrate the value of Six Sigma initiatives. Yellow Belts use these skills to monitor progress in their projects and report results to stakeholders.

How to Track Progress:

- Use Control Charts: Monitor key metrics over time to ensure process stability.
- Establish Performance Metrics: Define specific, measurable metrics (like defect rates or cycle times) to track improvements.

- Create a Reporting Schedule: Regularly update Green and Black Belts, as well as other stakeholders, on project progress, challenges, and results.

Example:
In a customer service project to reduce response times, a Yellow Belt might use a control chart to track average response time before and after implementing changes. They could also provide weekly progress reports to their supervisor.

Activity:
Have participants choose a simple process they'd like to improve and list two or three metrics they could track to monitor success.

Key Takeaways from Module 2

1. Yellow Belts play an active role in leading small projects and supporting larger initiatives led by higher-level belts.
2. They are responsible for data collection, root cause analysis, and tracking improvements, all essential tasks for successful Six Sigma projects.
3. Effective communication and teamwork are crucial, as Yellow Belts often collaborate with others and help build a Six Sigma culture within their team.
4. Promoting a Six Sigma culture involves encouraging data-driven decision-making, recognising achievements, and guiding White Belts.

Activity for Module 2: Reflection and Goal Setting

Objective: Help participants think about how they'll use their Yellow Belt skills and what specific responsibilities they can take on in their roles.

Instructions:

1. Have participants reflect on the responsibilities they feel most confident about and areas where they want to improve.
2. Ask them to set one or two specific goals for how they plan to apply their Yellow Belt knowledge and skills within their teams.

Example Goals:

- A participant in logistics might set a goal to lead a small project on reducing delivery times, using the DMAIC approach.
- A participant in retail could aim to provide better data support to a Green Belt-led project, helping track customer satisfaction metrics.

Module 3: Deeper Dive into DMAIC

Course Objective for Module 3

By the end of this module, participants should have a detailed understanding of each phase in the DMAIC process. They will learn how to use specific tools and techniques in each phase to manage small projects effectively and support larger Six Sigma initiatives.

---

1. Define Phase

Objective: Clearly identify the problem, set specific goals, and determine the project's scope. This phase also focuses on understanding the needs and expectations of the customer.

Key Activities:

1. Develop a Project Charter: Create a document that outlines the problem, project goals, scope, timeline, and team members. The Project Charter serves as a roadmap for the project.
2. Identify Critical to Quality (CTQ) Requirements: Understand what is most important to the customer and ensure that project goals align with these requirements.
3. Stakeholder Identification and Analysis: Identify who will be impacted by the project and involve them as needed.
4. Voice of the Customer (VoC): Collect customer feedback to define what quality means to the customer.

Example Tool:
SIPOC Diagram (Suppliers, Inputs, Process, Outputs, Customers) - A SIPOC diagram provides a high-level view of the process and helps teams understand how inputs affect outputs.

Activity:
Ask participants to create a simple Project Charter for a small project in their work area. This helps them practice defining project goals, scope, and identifying stakeholders.

---

2. Measure Phase

Objective: Gather data to understand the current state of the process, establish a baseline, and quantify the problem. This phase ensures that the team has a factual understanding of the process's current performance.

Key Activities:

1. Define Key Metrics and KPIs: Select relevant metrics that align with project goals, such as defect rate, cycle time, or customer satisfaction.
2. Data Collection Plan: Develop a structured plan that outlines what data to collect, how to collect it, and when.
3. Establish a Baseline: Use collected data to determine the current performance of the process. This baseline will help measure improvements later.
4. Measurement System Analysis (MSA): Ensure that data collection methods and measurement tools are accurate and reliable.

Example Tool:
Gage Repeatability and Reproducibility (Gage R&R) - Gage R&R
evaluates the consistency of measurement systems, ensuring
that data is reliable.

Activity:
Ask participants to outline a data collection plan for a specific
process in their area. This plan should include what they will
measure, the methods they'll use, and how often data will be
collected.

---

3. Analyse Phase

Objective: Identify the root causes of the problem by analysing
data and looking for patterns, bottlenecks, and sources of
variation. This phase aims to go beyond symptoms and address
the underlying causes of issues.

Key Activities:

1. Process Mapping: Use detailed process maps to
   understand each step and identify areas where delays,
   errors, or redundancies occur.
2. Root Cause Analysis: Use tools like the 5 Whys or
   Fishbone Diagram to drill down into the root causes of
   the problem.
3. Data Analysis: Review collected data to identify
   patterns, trends, or specific areas with high variation.
4. Hypothesis Testing: Test hypotheses about potential
   causes to confirm which factors are truly impacting the
   process.

Example Tool:
Fishbone Diagram (Cause and Effect Diagram) - This tool helps brainstorm and categorise possible causes of a problem, enabling teams to identify root causes.

Activity:
Ask participants to choose a recurring issue in their area and use a Fishbone Diagram to explore possible causes. This activity helps them practice root cause analysis.

---

4. Improve Phase

Objective: Develop, implement, and test solutions that address the root causes identified in the Analyse phase. This phase focuses on making changes to improve the process and eliminate issues.

Key Activities:

1. Brainstorming Solutions: Generate a list of potential solutions and evaluate them based on feasibility and impact.
2. Pilot Testing: Implement solutions on a small scale to test their effectiveness before full-scale implementation.
3. Solution Selection and Prioritisation: Use tools to prioritise solutions based on factors like cost, time, and expected impact.
4. Implementation Plan: Develop a clear plan for implementing the selected solution, including necessary training and resources.

Example Tool:
Solution Prioritisation Matrix - This matrix helps assess the feasibility and impact of each solution, making it easier to choose the best options.

Activity:
Ask participants to outline a pilot test plan for a solution to a problem in their area. This plan should include the steps they'll take, the metrics they'll measure, and the timeline for the test.

---

5. Control Phase

Objective: Ensure that improvements are maintained over time by establishing control mechanisms and monitoring the process. This phase prevents the process from returning to its previous state.

Key Activities:

1. Develop Control Plans: Define how the improved process will be monitored to ensure it remains stable and effective.
2. Establish Standard Operating Procedures (SOPs): Document the improved process to ensure it is consistently followed.
3. Implement Control Charts: Use control charts to track process performance and detect any deviations from expected results.
4. Ongoing Monitoring and Reporting: Set up regular checks and reporting systems to ensure the process stays within acceptable limits.

Example Tool:
Control Chart - This chart helps monitor process stability over time and alerts the team to any variations that might need attention.

Activity:
Ask participants to create a simple control plan for an improvement they want to sustain. This plan should include the metrics they'll monitor, the frequency of checks, and any corrective actions they'll take if performance deviates.

Practical Example of DMAIC in Action

To reinforce the DMAIC phases, here's an example of a simple Six Sigma project that a Yellow Belt might lead.

Scenario: Reducing Order Processing Time in a Small E-commerce Company

1. Define: The problem is that customers are experiencing long wait times for order confirmation. The project goal is to reduce order processing time by 25% within three months.
2. Measure: The Yellow Belt gathers data on current processing times and establishes that the average time from order placement to confirmation is 2 hours.
3. Analyse: The Yellow Belt uses a process map and Fishbone Diagram to identify that delays occur primarily during manual data entry.
4. Improve: The Yellow Belt introduces an automated data entry tool and runs a pilot test to see if processing times decrease.

5. Control: The Yellow Belt monitors order processing times weekly, using a control chart to ensure the improvement is maintained.

Outcome: By following DMAIC, the Yellow Belt successfully reduces the order processing time, leading to higher customer satisfaction and improved efficiency.

---

6. Activity: Apply DMAIC to a Small Project

Objective: Reinforce participants' understanding of DMAIC by having them apply each phase to a hypothetical or real-life project in their area.

Instructions:

1. Divide participants into small groups and have each group select a minor issue they want to address.
2. Have them outline each phase of DMAIC for their chosen issue, including specific activities and tools they would use.
3. Each group presents their DMAIC plan to the class for feedback and discussion.

Outcome: This activity provides practical experience with DMAIC, helping participants feel more confident about using this methodology to lead small projects.

Key Takeaways from Module 3

1. DMAIC provides a structured, step-by-step approach to problem-solving, helping Yellow Belts lead projects and improve processes.
2. Each phase of DMAIC has specific goals and activities: Define sets the problem, Measure collects data, Analyse identifies root causes, Improve implements solutions, and Control ensures sustainability.
3. Yellow Belts should be proficient in using tools like SIPOC diagrams, Fishbone Diagrams, Control Charts, and Solution Prioritisation Matrices to support each phase.
4. The DMAIC process can be applied to a wide range of issues, from reducing defects and cycle times to improving customer satisfaction.

Reflection Activity for Module 3

Objective: Help participants reflect on their understanding of DMAIC and identify any phases they feel less confident about.

Instructions:

1. Ask participants to consider which DMAIC phase they feel most comfortable with and which one they'd like to review further.
2. Encourage them to write down one specific goal for each phase, such as "improve data collection skills in the Measure phase" or "practice using Control Charts in the Control phase."

Outcome: This reflection helps participants take ownership of their learning and identify areas where they may need additional support or practice.

Module 4: Advanced Six Sigma Tools for Yellow Belts

Course Objective for Module 4
By the end of this module, participants will be familiar with advanced Six Sigma tools that allow for deeper analysis and more structured problem-solving. These tools enable Yellow Belts to better understand processes, identify root causes, assess risks, and prioritise solutions effectively.

---

1. Cause-and-Effect Matrix

Objective: Learn how to use the Cause-and-Effect Matrix to prioritise potential causes of a problem based on their impact on Critical to Quality (CTQ) factors.

Definition:
The Cause-and-Effect Matrix is a tool that helps prioritise causes by evaluating how strongly they influence CTQ requirements. This matrix is particularly useful when multiple factors might be contributing to a problem, helping the team focus on the most impactful causes.

How to Use the Cause-and-Effect Matrix:

1. List CTQ Requirements: Identify the factors that are critical to meeting customer needs.
2. List Potential Causes: Identify possible causes or inputs in the process that could affect the CTQs.
3. Assign Ratings: Rate each cause on a scale to determine its impact on each CTQ.

4. Calculate Total Scores: Add up scores to identify which causes have the highest impact, guiding focus on these areas for improvement.

Example:
In a hospital, a Yellow Belt might use a Cause-and-Effect Matrix to identify the main factors affecting patient wait times. By prioritising causes, they could determine that delays in patient handovers have the greatest impact, focusing their improvement efforts there.

Activity:
Provide participants with a sample Cause-and-Effect Matrix template and ask them to fill it out for a hypothetical issue, such as factors affecting delivery speed in a retail setting.

---

2. Failure Modes and Effects Analysis (FMEA)

Objective: Understand how to use FMEA to identify potential process failures and assess their impact, probability, and detectability.

Definition:
FMEA is a structured approach to identifying potential failure modes in a process, assessing the risks associated with each, and prioritising them for action. FMEA helps prevent issues before they occur, making it a proactive approach to quality management.

How to Use FMEA:

1. Identify Failure Modes: List potential ways each step of a process could fail.
2. Evaluate Impact, Probability, and Detectability: Rate each failure mode on a scale for each category.
3. Calculate Risk Priority Number (RPN): Multiply the scores for impact, probability, and detectability to get an RPN.
4. Prioritise and Take Action: Address the highest-risk failure modes by developing countermeasures or preventive actions.

Example:
In a manufacturing setting, a Yellow Belt could use FMEA to assess risks in a product assembly line. If they identify that a specific machine frequently causes defects, they could implement regular maintenance checks to reduce the likelihood of failure.

Activity:
Provide a sample FMEA worksheet and have participants practice filling it out for a process in their area, identifying potential failure modes and assigning RPNs.

---

3. Process Capability Analysis

Objective: Learn to assess whether a process is capable of meeting customer specifications consistently.

Definition:
Process Capability Analysis evaluates how well a process can meet specified limits. It involves calculating capability indices,

such as Cp and Cpk, which indicate the process's ability to produce outcomes within the desired specifications.

How to Perform Process Capability Analysis:

1. Define Specification Limits: Identify the upper and lower limits for the process based on customer requirements.
2. Collect Data: Gather data on the process's performance to calculate its mean and standard deviation.
3. Calculate Cp and Cpk:
   - Cp measures the process spread relative to the specification limits.
   - Cpk takes the process mean into account, showing if the process is centred within the limits.

Interpretation:

- Cp > 1.33: The process is generally capable.
- Cp < 1: The process needs improvement.

Example:
In a call centre, a Yellow Belt might use Process Capability Analysis to assess whether average call response times are consistently within acceptable limits. If the Cp or Cpk is low, they could investigate factors affecting response times and make necessary adjustments.

Activity:
Have participants calculate basic Cp and Cpk values using sample data, helping them understand the process's current capability.

4. Hypothesis Testing Basics

Objective: Introduce Yellow Belts to basic hypothesis testing concepts to confirm or refute assumptions about process performance.

Definition:
Hypothesis testing is a statistical method used to evaluate assumptions about a process. It helps determine whether observed data reflects real changes or is due to chance, guiding decision-making based on data.

Key Concepts:

1. Null Hypothesis (H0): The assumption that there is no significant difference or effect.
2. Alternative Hypothesis (H1): The assumption that there is a significant difference or effect.
3. p-Value: Indicates the probability of obtaining results at least as extreme as the observed data, assuming the null hypothesis is true.

Common Types of Tests:

- t-Test: Compares the means of two groups.
- ANOVA: Compares the means of multiple groups.
- Chi-Square Test: Tests relationships between categorical variables.

Example:
In a restaurant, a Yellow Belt might use a t-test to compare average customer wait times before and after a new process is

implemented, determining whether the change significantly reduced wait times.

Activity:
Provide a simple dataset and guide participants through a t-test to see if there is a significant difference between two groups.

---

5. Control Charts

Objective: Learn how to use Control Charts to monitor process stability over time and detect variations.

Definition:
Control Charts are graphical tools that track data points over time, with control limits indicating expected variation. Control Charts help determine whether a process is stable (in control) or if unusual factors are causing variations (out of control).

How to Use Control Charts:

1. Collect Data: Track a specific metric over time, such as cycle time or defect rate.
2. Plot Data Points: Plot each data point on the chart in time sequence.
3. Add Control Limits: Draw upper and lower control limits (typically set at ±3 standard deviations from the mean).
4. Interpret: Look for data points outside control limits or patterns, such as runs or shifts, that indicate special cause variation.

Example:
In a packaging facility, a Yellow Belt could use a Control Chart
to track the daily defect rate. If they notice data points
consistently trending upwards, this could indicate an emerging
issue that needs further investigation.

Activity:
Have participants plot sample data on a Control Chart and
interpret whether the process appears stable or if special
causes are impacting it.

---

6. Pareto Analysis for Problem Prioritisation

Objective: Use Pareto Analysis to identify and focus on the
"vital few" causes of problems based on the 80/20 rule.

Definition:
Pareto Analysis, based on the 80/20 principle, helps identify
the top causes of problems, focusing improvement efforts
where they will have the greatest impact. A Pareto Chart
visually represents causes in descending order of frequency or
impact.

Steps for Pareto Analysis:

1. Identify Issues: List potential causes or problems and
   collect data on their frequency or impact.
2. Sort by Frequency: Arrange issues in descending order
   of frequency or impact.
3. Calculate Cumulative Impact: Show the cumulative
   effect of each cause.

4. Plot the Pareto Chart: Create a bar chart showing the issues and a line chart for cumulative percentage.

Example:
In a tech support centre, a Yellow Belt might use Pareto Analysis to identify the most common customer issues. If 80% of complaints come from only three main issues, the team can focus on addressing those first.

Activity:
Have participants create a simple Pareto Chart for a list of issues, such as reasons for product returns in a retail setting.

---

7. Activity: Selecting and Applying Advanced Tools

Objective: Reinforce participants' understanding of when to use each advanced tool and how to apply it to real-world scenarios.

Instructions:

1. Divide participants into small groups and assign each group a hypothetical process improvement scenario (e.g., reducing lead time in a service department).
2. Ask each group to select the tools they would use at different stages of their project (e.g., FMEA for risk assessment, Control Charts for monitoring).
3. Have each group present their chosen tools and explain how they would apply them to achieve process improvement.

Outcome: This activity provides participants with practical experience in selecting the appropriate tools based on the nature of the problem.

Key Takeaways from Module 4

1. Advanced tools help Yellow Belts conduct deeper analysis and prioritise issues, providing a structured approach to solving complex problems.
2. Tools like Cause-and-Effect Matrices, FMEA, and Process Capability Analysis help identify and prioritise causes, assess risks, and evaluate whether processes meet customer requirements.
3. Control Charts and Pareto Analysis support process monitoring and problem prioritisation, helping teams focus on the most impactful improvements.
4. Hypothesis Testing provides statistical validation, allowing Yellow Belts to confirm or refute assumptions based on data.

Reflection Activity for Module 4

Objective: Help participants reflect on the advanced tools they feel most confident using and identify any tools they want to practice further.

Instructions:

1. Ask participants to rate their confidence level for each tool and identify one or two they feel less comfortable with.
2. Encourage them to write down specific goals for practicing these tools, such as applying FMEA to a work process or creating a Control Chart with real data.

Outcome: This reflection helps participants focus on their development areas and take ownership of their skills in using advanced Six Sigma tools.

Module 5: Leading a Small Six Sigma Project

Course Objective for Module 5
By the end of this module, participants should feel confident leading small Six Sigma projects in their own departments. They'll learn how to select a project, assemble a team, and use the DMAIC process to guide improvement efforts from start to finish.

---

1. Identifying a Suitable Project

Objective: Help participants choose a project that is achievable at the Yellow Belt level, has a clear focus, and is likely to bring meaningful improvements within a specific area.

Key Characteristics of a Good Yellow Belt Project:

- Narrow Scope: Projects should focus on a single department or process and be manageable within a short time frame (e.g., 1-3 months).
- Specific Problem: The problem should be clearly defined, such as reducing defect rates or decreasing cycle time in one area.
- Measurable Goals: The project should have clear, quantifiable objectives, like reducing errors by 20% or increasing process efficiency by 15%.
- Customer Impact: Projects should aim to improve quality, efficiency, or satisfaction for internal or external customers.

Example of a Suitable Project:
In a customer service team, a Yellow Belt might lead a project to reduce average call resolution time. This project has a narrow scope, a specific and measurable goal, and a clear impact on customer satisfaction.

Activity:
Ask participants to brainstorm potential projects in their areas, considering which problems are achievable within a short timeframe and have a measurable impact.

---

2. Defining the Project Scope and Goals

Objective: Teach participants how to set clear project boundaries and define measurable goals, ensuring the project remains focused and achievable.

Steps for Defining Project Scope:

1. Identify Project Boundaries: Specify which part of the process will be improved and any elements that are outside the project's scope.
2. Define Objectives: Set clear, quantifiable goals that align with Critical to Quality (CTQ) factors.
3. Establish a Timeline: Set a realistic timeframe for completing the project, typically 1-3 months.
4. Determine Resources Needed: Identify any resources (such as team members, tools, or budget) that the project requires.

Example:
For a project aiming to reduce order processing time in a retail

warehouse, the project scope might include the time from order placement to packaging but exclude shipping time. A specific goal could be to reduce order processing time by 20%.

Activity:
Have participants draft a brief project scope and goals for their chosen project, specifying what's included and excluded and defining clear objectives.

---

3. Assembling the Project Team

Objective: Guide Yellow Belts in selecting team members who can support the project effectively, with an emphasis on collaboration and role clarity.

Team Roles and Responsibilities:

1. Yellow Belt Leader: Responsible for managing the project, keeping it on track, and applying DMAIC principles.
2. Subject Matter Experts (SMEs): Provide insights into specific process areas and help identify potential causes of issues.
3. Data Collectors: Assist in gathering and recording data throughout the project.
4. Team Members: Support various phases of the project, participate in brainstorming, and help implement changes.

How to Select Team Members:

- Choose people who understand the process well and can provide relevant insights.
- Include team members from different functions if the project affects multiple areas.
- Aim for a team size of 3-5 members to keep meetings and collaboration manageable.

Example:
For a project to improve accuracy in stock-taking, a Yellow Belt might include a warehouse supervisor (SME), two data collectors, and a team member who regularly handles inventory.

Activity:
Ask participants to list potential team members for their project and define each person's role, ensuring they understand how to assemble an effective team.

---

4. Managing the DMAIC Phases for a Small Project

This section provides an overview of how Yellow Belts can apply each DMAIC phase to manage their project, with practical tips and considerations for each phase.

Define Phase

- Identify the Problem: Ensure the problem is clearly defined and aligned with customer needs.
- Create the Project Charter: Document project objectives, scope, and team members.

- Voice of the Customer (VoC): Collect insights from customers or stakeholders to ensure the project addresses their needs.

Tip: Keep the Project Charter simple and concise for small projects, focusing on core details like objectives and expected outcomes.

Measure Phase

- Establish Baseline Metrics: Gather data on the current performance of the process to measure improvements later.
- Define Key Metrics: Choose metrics that directly relate to the project goals, such as defect rate or cycle time.
- Create a Data Collection Plan: Define how and when data will be collected to ensure accuracy.

Tip: Use basic tools like Check Sheets to simplify data collection and ensure consistency.

Analyse Phase

- Identify Root Causes: Use tools like the Fishbone Diagram or 5 Whys to identify the underlying causes of the problem.
- Review Process Maps: Create or update process maps to understand the process flow and identify potential areas for improvement.
- Prioritise Causes: Focus on the main contributors to the problem, prioritising those that have the greatest impact.

Tip: Keep analysis focused and avoid over-complicating with excessive data; focus on identifying clear causes of the issue.

Improve Phase

- Brainstorm Solutions: Generate a list of potential solutions and evaluate them based on feasibility and impact.
- Pilot Testing: Implement a small-scale pilot test to see how the solution affects the process.
- Create an Implementation Plan: Once the solution is validated, develop a clear plan for full implementation.

Tip: Engage team members in brainstorming and testing, as their insights can lead to practical and effective solutions.

Control Phase

- Develop Control Measures: Define how the improvements will be monitored over time.
- Document New Processes: Update Standard Operating Procedures (SOPs) or create job aids to ensure consistency.
- Use Control Charts: Track performance metrics to ensure the process remains stable and improvements are sustained.

Tip: Regularly check the metrics even after implementation to ensure the solution remains effective.

Activity:
Have participants create a brief outline for each DMAIC phase based on their chosen project, highlighting key activities and tools they plan to use.

---

5. Communicating Project Progress and Results

Objective: Teach Yellow Belts how to provide clear and concise updates on project progress to stakeholders, team members, and higher-level belts.

Best Practices for Project Communication:

1. Set a Communication Schedule: Determine when and how updates will be shared (e.g., weekly emails or monthly meetings).
2. Use Simple, Clear Language: Avoid jargon and ensure updates are easy to understand for all stakeholders.
3. Highlight Key Metrics and Results: Focus on the impact of improvements, using data to demonstrate progress.
4. Celebrate Milestones: Recognise achievements, such as reaching a target or completing a phase, to keep the team motivated.

Example:
For a project to reduce equipment downtime, a Yellow Belt might provide weekly updates on the average downtime, current phase, and any adjustments made based on team feedback.

Activity:
Ask participants to draft a sample update for their project, including current phase, key metrics, and any challenges they're addressing.

---

6. Sustaining and Standardising Improvements

Objective: Teach participants how to maintain and standardise improvements to ensure long-term success after the project is complete.

Key Steps to Sustain Improvements:

1. Develop SOPs and Training Materials: Document the new process in SOPs or job aids to ensure consistency.
2. Assign Process Owners: Designate team members responsible for monitoring and maintaining the improvements.
3. Conduct Regular Check-Ins: Schedule periodic reviews to ensure the process remains stable and improvements are upheld.
4. Gather Feedback for Continuous Improvement: Encourage team members to provide feedback on the process for ongoing refinement.

Example:
In a retail store, a Yellow Belt might create a checklist and SOP for managing product returns, assigning a process owner to ensure adherence and providing periodic updates on metrics like return processing time.

Activity:
Have participants outline a simple control plan for sustaining their project improvements, detailing SOPs, monitoring metrics, and process owner responsibilities.

Key Takeaways from Module 5

1. Yellow Belts can effectively lead small projects using the DMAIC process, focusing on specific improvements within their departments.
2. Defining clear project goals and scope helps keep projects focused, manageable, and aligned with customer needs.
3. Assembling the right team and applying DMAIC tools at each phase are essential to project success.
4. Effective communication ensures that team members and stakeholders stay informed, helping sustain motivation and support for the project.
5. Documenting and monitoring improvements are key to sustaining long-term success and maintaining Six Sigma culture.

Reflection Activity for Module 5

Objective: Help participants reflect on their readiness to lead a project and identify any areas where they might need further support or resources.

Instructions:

1. Ask participants to consider which DMAIC phase they feel most prepared to manage and which phase they'd like to review or practice further.
2. Encourage them to set a specific goal for leading a project, such as creating an action plan or practising communication skills.

Outcome: This reflection helps participants take ownership of their learning and builds confidence for leading small Six Sigma projects.

Module 6: Supporting Green and Black Belts

Course Objective for Module 6

By the end of this module, participants will understand their role in supporting Green and Black Belts during larger Six Sigma projects. They will learn specific ways they can contribute to the project's success by gathering data, providing insights, assisting with implementation, and promoting a culture of continuous improvement.

---

1. Understanding the Green and Black Belt Roles

Objective: Provide an overview of the responsibilities of Green and Black Belts, helping Yellow Belts understand where they fit in the project hierarchy.

Overview of Responsibilities:

- Green Belts: Lead department-level projects and manage data analysis, root cause identification, and solution implementation. They may also support Black Belt-led projects by focusing on specific areas.
- Black Belts: Manage cross-functional projects, drive strategic initiatives, and use advanced Six Sigma tools to solve complex problems. Black Belts oversee all project phases, including high-level data analysis, strategy alignment, and team coordination.

Where Yellow Belts Fit:

Yellow Belts provide essential support in data collection,

process observation, implementation, and reporting. By collaborating with Green and Black Belts, they contribute valuable frontline insights and help maintain communication within the team.

Activity:
Ask participants to reflect on a project in their area and identify which parts could benefit from Green or Black Belt support. This exercise helps them understand the areas where higher-level belts provide expertise.

---

2. Data Collection and Reporting

Objective: Teach Yellow Belts how to collect and report data effectively, providing Green and Black Belts with accurate information for analysis.

Best Practices for Data Collection:

1. Define What to Measure: Collaborate with the Green or Black Belt to ensure the data collected aligns with the project goals.
2. Use Consistent Methods: Follow standardised data collection techniques to ensure accuracy and reliability.
3. Document Procedures: Keep records of data collection methods, tools used, and any conditions that could impact results.
4. Check for Consistency: Regularly review the data to identify any inconsistencies or potential sources of error.

Reporting Data:

- Organise Data Clearly: Use tables, charts, or graphs to present data in an easy-to-understand format.
- Summarise Key Points: Highlight important trends or patterns in the data that could inform the project direction.
- Provide Context: Include details about the conditions under which the data was collected (e.g., time of day, staff levels) to aid interpretation.

Example:
In a hospital project to reduce patient wait times, a Yellow Belt might collect data on patient check-in and triage times. By presenting this data in a control chart, they help the Green Belt identify patterns or trends that contribute to delays.

Activity:
Ask participants to think of a metric they could collect for a current process. Have them outline a brief data collection plan, specifying what data to collect, how to collect it, and how they would report the results.

---

3. Conducting Process Observations

Objective: Teach Yellow Belts how to observe processes effectively, identifying inefficiencies, bottlenecks, and opportunities for improvement.

Steps for Conducting Process Observations:

1. Clarify the Objective: Understand what the Green or Black Belt is looking to improve so that observations are focused and relevant.

2. Watch for Bottlenecks: Identify steps in the process where tasks or people wait, which may indicate inefficiencies.
3. Note Variability: Observe any variations in how the process is completed, such as different approaches used by different staff members.
4. Document Findings: Record observations clearly, noting any patterns or potential causes of inefficiencies.

Example:
In a retail store, a Yellow Belt might observe the checkout process to identify delays. If they notice that price checks are causing slowdowns, they can report this to the Green Belt, who may explore solutions like better pricing information.

Activity:
Have participants outline a process in their work area that they could observe. Ask them to list specific elements they would look for, such as bottlenecks or variations, and consider how they might record their observations.

---

4. Supporting Implementation Efforts

Objective: Teach Yellow Belts how to assist Green and Black Belts with implementing solutions, ensuring that changes are adopted smoothly and consistently.

Ways Yellow Belts Can Support Implementation:

1. Participate in Pilot Testing: Help conduct small-scale tests of proposed solutions, providing feedback on their practicality and effectiveness.

2. Assist with Training: Help train colleagues on new procedures or tools, ensuring they understand the changes and how to follow them correctly.
3. Monitor Compliance: Observe whether team members are following the new processes consistently and provide feedback to the project lead.
4. Gather Feedback: Collect insights from frontline staff on how the changes are working in practice, reporting any issues or suggestions for refinement.

Example:
In a restaurant, a Yellow Belt might help implement a new order-taking system to improve speed. They could assist with training staff on the new system, monitor how well it's being used, and report any difficulties back to the Green Belt.

Activity:
Ask participants to think of a recent change in their workplace. Have them list ways they could have supported the implementation, such as helping with training or monitoring compliance.

---

5. Providing Feedback on Solutions

Objective: Encourage Yellow Belts to offer constructive feedback during and after implementation, helping higher-level belts refine and adjust solutions as needed.

How to Provide Effective Feedback:

- Be Specific: Clearly describe any issues or successes observed, including when and where they occurred.

- Focus on Solutions: If challenges arise, suggest possible adjustments or improvements.
- Encourage Open Communication: Be open to discussing both successes and challenges with the team, promoting a culture of improvement.
- Follow Up: After providing feedback, follow up to see if the solution has improved or if further adjustments are needed.

Example:
In a project to improve call resolution times, a Yellow Belt might notice that the new procedure is effective for common issues but slows down when handling unique problems. They could suggest specific improvements to make the procedure more adaptable, helping the Green Belt refine the approach.

Activity:
Have participants think of a process change they've experienced and reflect on how they could have provided constructive feedback. This exercise helps them practice offering feedback in a way that supports continuous improvement.

---

6. Promoting a Continuous Improvement Mindset

Objective: Encourage Yellow Belts to foster a culture of continuous improvement within their teams, supporting Green and Black Belts by promoting positive attitudes and improvement-focused behaviours.

Ways Yellow Belts Can Promote Continuous Improvement:

1. Encourage Data Use: Help colleagues understand the value of data-driven decisions by explaining how data informs improvements.
2. Celebrate Small Wins: Recognise and celebrate incremental improvements to build morale and keep the team motivated.
3. Share Learning: Provide guidance to team members, helping them understand Six Sigma principles and how they can contribute.
4. Promote Open Dialogue: Encourage team members to share their observations and suggestions, fostering a collaborative improvement culture.

Example:
In a logistics department, a Yellow Belt might encourage colleagues to track delivery times and suggest small improvements, such as adjusting routes, to reduce delays. By promoting small changes, they help create a culture where everyone is invested in quality.

Activity:
Ask participants to list specific actions they can take to promote a continuous improvement mindset within their team. Discuss how these actions contribute to Six Sigma culture and support larger projects.

---

7. Acting as a Liaison Between Higher-Level Belts and Team Members

Objective: Help Yellow Belts understand their role as a communication link, keeping both the project team and their colleagues informed about project progress and challenges.

Responsibilities as a Liaison:

- Provide Updates to Higher Belts: Keep Green and Black Belts informed of any frontline issues, observations, or potential improvements.
- Communicate Project Goals to Team Members: Help colleagues understand the purpose of the project and how changes will benefit them.
- Address Team Concerns: Listen to team members' concerns about changes and relay these back to the project team, ensuring they are addressed.
- Encourage Engagement: Motivate team members to actively participate in improvements, fostering a sense of ownership and involvement.

Example:
In a healthcare setting, a Yellow Belt could act as a liaison in a project to reduce appointment wait times. They might communicate the project's progress to nurses and administrative staff, address any concerns, and relay frontline feedback to the Green Belt.

Activity:
Have participants outline a simple communication plan for sharing updates with their team and higher-level belts. This helps them practice effective communication as a liaison.

Key Takeaways from Module 6

1. Yellow Belts play a crucial support role in large Six Sigma projects, contributing through data collection,

process observations, and assisting with solution implementation.

2. Providing accurate data and reporting findings clearly are essential responsibilities, helping Green and Black Belts make informed decisions.
3. Promoting a continuous improvement mindset among team members supports Six Sigma culture, encouraging everyone to look for ways to enhance quality and efficiency.
4. Effective communication helps bridge the gap between higher-level belts and team members, ensuring everyone stays informed and engaged.

Reflection Activity for Module 6

Objective: Encourage participants to reflect on how they can apply these support skills in their current role.

Instructions:

1. Ask participants to think about which support activities (data collection, feedback, implementation support) they feel most comfortable with and which they'd like to practice further.
2. Have them write down specific goals for how they plan to assist Green and Black Belts on future projects, such as improving their data reporting skills or actively promoting continuous improvement.

Outcome: This reflection activity helps participants recognise their strengths and identify areas for development in supporting higher-level Six Sigma projects.

Module 7: Encouraging a Continuous Improvement Culture

Course Objective for Module 7

By the end of this module, participants will understand the importance of fostering a continuous improvement culture in the workplace. They will learn strategies to encourage team members, promote data-driven thinking, celebrate improvements, and sustain a mindset focused on quality and efficiency.

---

1. Understanding Continuous Improvement Culture

Objective: Help participants understand the core elements of a continuous improvement culture and its benefits for both employees and the organisation.

What is Continuous Improvement Culture?

- Mindset of Constant Development: Continuous improvement is a belief that every process, no matter how well it's functioning, has potential for improvement.
- Focus on Incremental Changes: Instead of waiting for big changes, a continuous improvement culture encourages small, incremental improvements over time.
- Data-Driven Decision Making: Continuous improvement relies on collecting and analysing data to guide changes, ensuring that improvements are based on evidence.

Benefits of Continuous Improvement Culture:

1. Enhanced Efficiency: Small changes accumulate to create streamlined, efficient processes.
2. Improved Quality: Incremental improvements lead to fewer defects, higher customer satisfaction, and better outcomes.
3. Engaged Employees: Employees feel more empowered when they're encouraged to suggest improvements and participate in problem-solving.
4. Adaptability: A culture that values improvement is more adaptable to change, helping teams stay competitive in a dynamic environment.

Example:
In a manufacturing plant, a continuous improvement culture might encourage employees to suggest ways to reduce setup time on machines. Small changes, such as reorganising tools or standardising procedures, can lead to significant efficiency gains.

Activity:
Ask participants to reflect on their current workplace culture and identify aspects that support or hinder continuous improvement. Discuss examples from each participant's experience to highlight the impact of a positive improvement culture.

---

2. Encouraging Data-Driven Thinking

Objective: Teach Yellow Belts how to promote the importance of data-driven decisions, helping their teams see data as a valuable resource for making improvements.

Strategies for Promoting Data-Driven Thinking:

1. Collect Data Regularly: Encourage teams to gather data consistently, even on small tasks, so there's always a factual basis for decisions.
2. Discuss Data Insights: Share data with the team, explaining how it relates to performance and pointing out trends or patterns.
3. Use Data to Set Goals: Base improvement goals on current data, showing team members how data supports objectives.
4. Recognise Data-Driven Suggestions: When team members make suggestions based on data, acknowledge their efforts to reinforce the importance of this approach.

Example:
In a sales team, a Yellow Belt might encourage colleagues to track their call-to-sale conversion rates. Reviewing this data helps them identify techniques that lead to better results and focus on actions that improve performance.

Activity:
Have participants choose a metric they think their team should track. Ask them to outline a simple data collection plan for tracking this metric, including who would collect the data, how often, and how it could be used to support decisions.

3. Promoting Small Improvements

Objective: Encourage Yellow Belts to advocate for small, manageable improvements that build up over time, creating a foundation for continuous improvement.

Why Small Improvements Matter:

- Easier to Implement: Small changes are less disruptive and easier to manage within daily tasks.
- Lower Cost: Small adjustments often require fewer resources, making them more practical.
- Boost Morale: Celebrating small wins keeps team morale high and encourages ongoing engagement with improvement initiatives.

Examples of Small Improvements:

1. Reducing Waste: Find small ways to reduce resource usage, such as switching to reusable materials or optimising workflows.
2. Streamlining Steps: Eliminate unnecessary steps in a process to save time and improve efficiency.
3. Improving Organisation: Simple changes, such as rearranging workspaces, can make tasks easier and faster to complete.

Example:
In an office environment, a Yellow Belt might notice that employees waste time searching for documents. Implementing a standardised file-naming system could help reduce time spent on this task.

Activity:

Ask participants to identify one small improvement they could implement in their area. Have them share how this change could impact their team's efficiency or quality of work.

---

4. Celebrating Achievements and Recognising Efforts

Objective: Show Yellow Belts how to recognise and celebrate improvements to maintain motivation and reinforce a culture of continuous improvement.

Strategies for Recognising Efforts:

1. Acknowledge Small Wins: Recognise even small improvements, as they contribute to long-term progress.
2. Highlight Team Contributions: Celebrate team members who have suggested changes or supported improvements.
3. Share Success Stories: Encourage team members to share their improvement stories, fostering a sense of accomplishment.
4. Provide Incentives: Small rewards or recognitions, such as a certificate or public acknowledgment, reinforce positive behaviours.

Example:

In a healthcare setting, a Yellow Belt might celebrate a team's improvement in patient check-in time by sharing the results at a team meeting. Recognising the team's role in making the improvement motivates them to continue looking for ways to enhance service.

Activity:
Ask participants to plan a simple way they could recognise a team member's contribution to a recent improvement, such as mentioning their effort in a team meeting or sending a thank-you email.

---

5. Engaging Team Members in Continuous Improvement

Objective: Encourage Yellow Belts to actively involve their team members in improvement efforts, creating a more collaborative environment.

Ways to Engage Team Members:

1. Ask for Input Regularly: Encourage team members to share their observations and suggestions for improvements.
2. Empower Team-Led Initiatives: Give team members ownership of small improvement projects to foster engagement.
3. Provide Learning Opportunities: Offer resources or training to help team members build their problem-solving skills.
4. Create Feedback Loops: Establish a system for team members to share their improvement ideas and receive feedback from the Yellow Belt or higher-level belts.

Example:
In a logistics company, a Yellow Belt could hold regular team meetings where employees are encouraged to suggest ways to

improve delivery times. By implementing some of their suggestions, the Yellow Belt shows that team input is valued.

Activity:
Have participants brainstorm one way they could engage their team members in an improvement effort. Encourage them to think about how they could facilitate team ownership of the process.

---

6. Building a Structured Approach to Improvements

Objective: Teach Yellow Belts how to implement a structured approach for identifying, prioritising, and tracking improvements, ensuring sustained progress.

Steps for a Structured Approach:

1. Identify Improvement Opportunities: Use tools like the Fishbone Diagram or Pareto Analysis to pinpoint areas with the most impact.
2. Prioritise Changes: Evaluate improvement ideas based on factors like feasibility, cost, and potential impact.
3. Develop an Action Plan: Set specific steps, deadlines, and responsibilities for implementing each improvement.
4. Monitor Progress: Track metrics to measure the effectiveness of the improvement and ensure it's sustained over time.

Example:
In a customer service department, a Yellow Belt might create an action plan to reduce call wait times. By tracking average

wait times each week, they can monitor whether the improvement is having the desired effect.

Activity:
Ask participants to outline a brief action plan for one small improvement in their area, including key steps, who would be involved, and how they would track progress.

---

7. Encouraging Problem-Solving Skills and Creativity

Objective: Show Yellow Belts how to foster problem-solving skills and creativity within their teams, encouraging innovative solutions.

Strategies to Encourage Problem-Solving:

1. Host Brainstorming Sessions: Encourage open discussions for team members to share ideas.
2. Promote Experimentation: Encourage teams to test new ideas on a small scale before fully implementing them.
3. Use the 5 Whys: Teach team members the 5 Whys technique to dig deeper into issues and find root causes.
4. Reward Creative Solutions: Recognise team members who come up with innovative solutions that add value.

Example:
In a retail store, a Yellow Belt might hold a brainstorming session to find ways to improve checkout efficiency. By letting team members experiment with different approaches, they may discover a faster checkout process.

Activity:

Ask participants to lead a simple brainstorming session with their team, focused on a specific challenge. Encourage them to apply techniques like the 5 Whys and reflect on the effectiveness of the session.

Key Takeaways from Module 7

1. Continuous improvement culture promotes quality, efficiency, and teamwork, creating an environment where employees feel engaged and motivated to make a difference.
2. Data-driven thinking and small incremental changes are at the core of continuous improvement, making it easier to identify opportunities and implement changes.
3. Recognising achievements and involving team members fosters a sense of ownership and collaboration, reinforcing the value of Six Sigma principles.
4. A structured approach to improvement ensures that changes are prioritised, implemented effectively, and monitored over time, supporting long-term success.

Reflection Activity for Module 7

Objective: Help participants reflect on their role in promoting continuous improvement and set personal goals for creating a positive improvement culture in their teams.

Instructions:

1. Ask participants to identify one area where they could start promoting a continuous improvement culture within their team.
2. Encourage them to set specific goals, such as regularly collecting data, recognising team achievements, or facilitating monthly improvement discussions.

Outcome: This reflection activity reinforces the idea that Yellow Belts play a critical role in fostering continuous improvement, giving them actionable steps to create a positive impact within their teams.

Module 8: Summary and Next Steps

Course Objective for Module 8
By the end of this module, participants will have a comprehensive understanding of the core concepts covered in the Yellow Belt course. They will reflect on their learning, set actionable goals, and explore opportunities for further development in Six Sigma, including advancing to Green Belt.

1. Review of Key Yellow Belt Concepts

Objective: Summarise the main topics covered throughout the course, ensuring participants feel confident about their knowledge and understanding.

Key Topics Recap:

1. What is Six Sigma?
   Six Sigma is a data-driven methodology aimed at improving processes by reducing variation and defects. The goal is to meet customer expectations with consistent, high-quality outputs.

2. DMAIC Methodology

- Define: Identify the problem and set clear project goals.
- Measure: Gather data and establish a baseline for process performance.
- Analyse: Identify root causes using tools such as the Fishbone Diagram and Pareto Analysis.

- Improve: Develop, test, and implement solutions to address root causes.
- Control: Put measures in place to sustain improvements.

3. Yellow Belt Responsibilities
   Yellow Belts lead small improvement projects, support Green and Black Belts, promote continuous improvement, and act as a link between Six Sigma projects and their teams.

4. Advanced Tools
   Yellow Belts use advanced tools such as the Cause-and-Effect Matrix, FMEA, and Control Charts to analyse and improve processes.

5. Continuous Improvement Culture
   A Six Sigma culture encourages ongoing improvement, data-driven decision-making, and employee engagement. Yellow Belts play a key role in fostering this mindset within their teams.

Activity:
Have participants complete a brief quiz or reflection exercise where they summarise each concept in their own words, reinforcing their understanding and retention of key topics.

2. Applying Yellow Belt Knowledge in Daily Work

Objective: Help participants plan specific ways to apply their new skills in their current roles, focusing on practical improvements and collaboration with their teams.

Practical Applications of Yellow Belt Skills:

1. Identify Improvement Opportunities: Look for small areas within daily tasks that could benefit from increased efficiency or reduced variation.
2. Data Collection and Analysis: Apply data collection techniques to track performance, identify patterns, and make data-driven decisions.
3. Use Six Sigma Tools: Use tools like Check Sheets, Process Flow Diagrams, and Control Charts to gather insights and manage improvement efforts.
4. Lead Small Projects: Select a manageable issue in the workplace and use the DMAIC process to lead an improvement project.

Example:
A Yellow Belt in a retail store might lead a project to streamline the product restocking process. By tracking restocking times and analysing patterns, they could identify ways to reduce delays and improve efficiency.

Activity:
Ask participants to write down one specific process in their work area where they could apply a Six Sigma tool or lead a small improvement project. This helps them think practically about their new skills.

---

3. Setting Personal Improvement Goals

Objective: Encourage participants to set achievable goals for using their Yellow Belt skills and contributing to a culture of continuous improvement.

Steps to Set Personal Goals:

1. Identify Areas for Growth: Consider which aspects of Six Sigma they would like to develop further, such as leading projects or using advanced tools.
2. Define Clear Objectives: Set specific, measurable goals, such as reducing error rates by a certain percentage or improving process efficiency within a set timeframe.
3. Set a Timeline: Determine a realistic timeline for achieving each goal, helping them stay focused and motivated.
4. Review Progress: Regularly assess progress toward goals, adjusting plans as needed to stay on track.

Example Goals:

- A Yellow Belt in healthcare might set a goal to reduce patient wait times by 10% over the next three months.
- A Yellow Belt in customer service could aim to improve first-call resolution rates by 15% within a month.

Activity:
Have participants create a personal action plan for the next three months, including their specific goals, the tools they will use, and how they will track progress.

---

4. Advancing to Green Belt

Objective: Provide participants with information on the Green Belt level and the additional skills and responsibilities it entails, encouraging those interested to pursue further certification.

Overview of Green Belt Responsibilities:

- Lead Larger Projects: Green Belts manage more complex projects that impact multiple areas or processes.
- Data Analysis and Root Cause Investigation: They perform detailed analysis, using statistical methods and advanced Six Sigma tools to identify and address issues.
- Project Management: Green Belts have a higher level of project management responsibility, including planning, team coordination, and communication with stakeholders.
- Mentoring Yellow Belts: Green Belts often support Yellow Belts by providing guidance on projects, helping build a strong Six Sigma culture within the team.

Benefits of Advancing to Green Belt:

- Enhanced Problem-Solving Skills: Gain deeper knowledge of Six Sigma tools and techniques.
- Career Advancement: Green Belt certification can open up opportunities for career growth in quality management and process improvement.
- Broader Impact: Green Belts have a greater impact on organisational success by leading cross-functional projects that drive meaningful change.

Activity:
Encourage participants to reflect on whether they're interested

in pursuing Green Belt certification. Ask them to consider what additional skills or knowledge they hope to gain and discuss how Green Belt training could support their career goals.

---

5. Resources for Continued Learning

Objective: Provide participants with resources to continue building their Six Sigma knowledge, encouraging them to stay engaged with continuous improvement practices.

Recommended Resources:

1. Books: Suggested titles include **The Lean Six Sigma Pocket Toolbook**, **Six Sigma for Managers**, and **The Lean Six Sigma Guide to Doing More with Less**.
2. Online Courses: Websites like Coursera, Udemy, and ASQ (American Society for Quality) offer Six Sigma and Lean courses.
3. Software Tools: Learning tools such as Minitab, JMP, or SigmaXL can enhance data analysis skills, allowing for more sophisticated process assessments.
4. Mentorship Opportunities: Encourage participants to seek mentorship from Green or Black Belts in their organisation, providing guidance and support for ongoing learning.

Example:
A participant interested in developing data analysis skills might take an online course on statistical analysis using Minitab, gaining hands-on experience with software commonly used in Six Sigma projects.

Activity:

Ask participants to choose one resource they plan to explore further, helping them create a personal development plan for building on their Yellow Belt training.

---

6. Creating a Personal Action Plan

Objective: Help participants develop a clear plan for applying their Yellow Belt skills in their roles, with a focus on continuous improvement and measurable outcomes.

Steps to Create an Action Plan:

1. Identify Immediate Applications: Choose one or two ways they can apply what they've learned right away, such as leading a small project or tracking performance data.
2. Set Improvement Goals: Define specific, achievable goals for the next 3-6 months, focusing on measurable outcomes.
3. Choose Relevant Tools: Select the Six Sigma tools that will be most useful for achieving each goal.
4. Monitor and Review Progress: Decide how they'll track their progress and when they'll review the impact of these improvements.
5. Seek Feedback: Encourage participants to ask for feedback from colleagues, supervisors, or mentors to refine their approach.

Example Action Plan:

A Yellow Belt in manufacturing might plan to use Control Charts to monitor defect rates, aiming to reduce defects by

10% over the next quarter. They could set monthly review sessions to evaluate progress and make adjustments as needed.

Activity:
Have participants draft a personal action plan that includes their immediate goals, tools, timeline, and review process. This action plan will help them take immediate, practical steps toward continuous improvement.

---

7. Celebrating Completion and Next Steps

Objective: Recognise participants' achievement in completing the Yellow Belt course and reinforce their value in supporting Six Sigma projects and culture.

Acknowledging Achievement:

- Certificate of Completion: Provide participants with a Yellow Belt certificate, formally recognising their accomplishment.
- Highlight Their Role: Emphasise the importance of Yellow Belts in Six Sigma projects, reinforcing their role in creating a continuous improvement culture.
- Celebrate as a Team: Encourage participants to share what they've learned with their colleagues, creating excitement around Six Sigma principles and inspiring others to get involved.

Encouraging Ongoing Engagement:

- Plan a Project: Encourage participants to begin their first Yellow Belt project, even a small one, to practice what they've learned.
- Seek Support: Remind participants to reach out to Green and Black Belts for guidance and mentorship as they apply their new skills.
- Continue Learning: Motivate participants to keep exploring Six Sigma and Lean principles, even informally, to reinforce their skills and build their expertise.

Final Activity:
Have participants share one specific goal they plan to achieve in the next six months using their Yellow Belt skills. This gives them a chance to set their intentions, receive feedback, and leave the course with a clear sense of purpose.

Key Takeaways from Module 8

1. Yellow Belt skills can be applied immediately in participants' roles, helping them identify improvement opportunities, lead small projects, and support Six Sigma culture.
2. Setting personal goals and a structured action plan provides a roadmap for success, helping Yellow Belts make meaningful contributions to their teams.
3. Ongoing learning and advancement opportunities, such as Green Belt certification, support continuous growth, allowing Yellow Belts to build on their knowledge and take on larger responsibilities.
4. Continuous improvement is a journey, and Yellow Belts are vital in supporting Six Sigma projects, fostering a

positive culture, and driving small but impactful changes in their organisations.

Reflection and Goal-Setting Activity for Module 8

Objective: Help participants reflect on their learning journey, set actionable goals, and solidify their next steps.

Instructions:

1. Ask participants to reflect on their favourite module, the most valuable concept they learned, and any remaining questions they may have.
2. Have them write down two specific goals they aim to achieve with their Yellow Belt skills, focusing on how they will apply their knowledge in their current roles.

Outcome: This reflection activity reinforces key concepts, gives participants a clear path forward, and helps them commit to using their Yellow Belt training in practical, measurable ways

6 Sigma Yellow Belt Course Handouts

Module 1: Introduction to Six Sigma

Learning Objectives:

- Understand what Six Sigma is and how it benefits an organisation.
- Learn about the DMAIC process and how it drives process improvement.
- Define the roles and responsibilities of a Yellow Belt in a Six Sigma project.

Key Terms:

- **Six Sigma**: A methodology aimed at improving process quality by reducing defects to 3.4 per million opportunities.
- **DMAIC**: The Six Sigma improvement methodology that stands for Define, Measure, Analyse, Improve, and Control.
- **Yellow Belt**: A person trained in the basics of Six Sigma who supports project teams in the implementation of process improvements.

Key Concepts:

1. **Six Sigma Methodology**: A structured, data-driven approach to eliminating defects and improving process performance.
2. **Yellow Belt's Role**: Yellow Belts typically assist Green Belts and Black Belts by collecting data, participating in process mapping, and identifying improvement areas.
3. **DMAIC Process**: The core process of Six Sigma that guides projects from problem definition to solution implementation.

Diagram: DMAIC Process
Here's a flowchart to visualise the DMAIC cycle:

```
In plaintext

[Define] → [Measure] → [Analyse] → [Improve] →
[Control]
```

Example: In a manufacturing environment, Six Sigma could help reduce the rate of defective products by identifying inefficiencies, eliminating causes of defects, and implementing robust controls.

Activity:
True or False

- The goal of Six Sigma is to eliminate all defects in processes. **(True)**
- Yellow Belts are responsible for leading projects. **(False)**

Module 2: Define Phase - Understanding the Problem

Learning Objectives:

- Learn how to define the problem clearly in the Define phase.
- Understand the tools used to capture customer needs and define project goals.

Key Terms:

- **Problem Statement**: A clear, concise description of the problem to be solved.
- **SIPOC Diagram**: A tool used to map the process flow, identifying Suppliers, Inputs, Process, Outputs, and Customers.
- **Project Charter**: A document that outlines the project's objectives, scope, and stakeholders.

Define Tools:

- **SIPOC Diagram**: A high-level process map that provides an overview of the system.

SIPOC Diagram:

In plaintext

Suppliers → Inputs → Process → Outputs → Customers

Key Concepts:

1. **Problem Statement**: The foundation of any Six Sigma project is to clearly define the problem being solved.
2. **Setting Project Goals**: Establishing measurable goals to track the success of the project.
3. **Stakeholder Identification**: Identifying key stakeholders and understanding their expectations.

Example: In a hospital, if patient waiting times are a concern, a project charter might be created to reduce wait times by 20% over six months.

Activity:
Create a SIPOC Diagram for a simple process (e.g., order processing). Identify the Suppliers, Inputs, Process, Outputs, and Customers involved.

Module 3: Measure Phase - Collecting Data

Learning Objectives:

- Understand the importance of data collection in the Measure phase.

- Learn how to identify relevant metrics and baseline performance.

Key Terms:

- **Baseline Data**: The current state of the process before any improvements are made.
- **Key Performance Indicators (KPIs)**: Metrics used to evaluate process performance.
- **Measurement System Analysis (MSA)**: An assessment to ensure the accuracy and reliability of data collection.

Measure Tools:

- **Data Collection Plan**: A document that outlines what data is needed and how it will be gathered.
- **Pareto Chart**: A bar chart used to identify the most significant factors contributing to a problem by prioritising them.

Pareto Chart Example:

In plaintext

```
|-----------------------------------------|
|          Top Issues in Process          |
|-----------------------------------------|
| Issue 1  | |██████████████████████████| |
| Issue 2  | |████████████████████|        |
| Issue 3  | |████████████|                |
|-----------------------------------------|
```

Key Concepts:

1. **Data Collection**: Accurate data is critical for understanding the current process performance.
2. **Defining Metrics**: Choose metrics that directly reflect the process performance and customer satisfaction.
3. **Measurement Tools**: Tools like control charts and histograms can help assess the variation and distribution of data.

Example: In a logistics company, baseline data might include the average delivery time for customer orders, which can be collected and tracked to measure improvements.

Activity:
Create a Data Collection Plan for a process you are familiar with (e.g., customer feedback). What data would you collect, and how would you gather it?

Module 4: Analyse Phase - Identifying Root Causes

Learning Objectives:

- Learn how to analyse data to identify the root causes of process issues.
- Understand the tools used to perform root cause analysis.

Key Terms:

- **Root Cause**: The primary cause of a problem, which, when solved, will prevent recurrence.
- **Fishbone Diagram**: A diagram used to identify potential causes of a problem by categorising them into groups like People, Processes, Machines, and Materials.
- **The 5 Whys**: A technique for identifying the root cause by asking "Why?" repeatedly.

Analyse Tools:

- **Fishbone Diagram (Ishikawa Diagram)**: Helps identify the causes of a problem in a structured way.
- **The 5 Whys**: Asking "Why?" five times to drill down to the underlying cause.

Fishbone Diagram Example:

```
In plaintext

      [Problem] --> [People] --> [Training Issues]
                    [Methods] --> [Process
Variability]
                    [Machines] --> [Outdated
Equipment]
                    [Materials] --> [Poor Quality
Raw Materials]
```

Key Concepts:

1. **Root Cause Analysis**: It's critical to address the root cause, not just the symptoms, of a problem.
2. **Data Analysis**: Statistical analysis helps to pinpoint the variables affecting process performance.
3. **The 5 Whys**: This technique is a simple, effective way to dig deeper into problems and identify root causes.

Example: In a restaurant, delays in food preparation might be traced to a root cause of insufficient staff training using the Fishbone Diagram and 5 Whys.

Activity:
Use the 5 Whys Technique to analyse a problem in your work (e.g., slow customer service). Ask "Why?" five times to uncover the root cause.

Module 5: Improve Phase - Implementing Solutions

Learning Objectives:

- Learn how to develop and implement solutions to address the root causes identified in the Analyse phase.
- Understand the importance of testing solutions before full implementation.

Key Terms:

- **Solution Implementation**: The process of applying the improvement strategies to the process.
- **Pilot Testing**: Running a small-scale test to validate the effectiveness of the solution.

Key Concepts:

1. **Designing Solutions**: Solutions should directly address the root causes of the problems identified.
2. **Pilot Testing**: Testing the solution in a limited setting before rolling it out more broadly.
3. **Risk Management**: Assessing potential risks associated with the solution and developing mitigation strategies.

Example: In a hospital, implementing a new patient check-in system could be tested in one department before being introduced hospital-wide.

Activity:
Design an Improvement Plan for a process you've worked on. What changes would you make, and how would you test them?

---

6 Sigma Yellow Belt Question Sheet

Section 1: True/False Questions

1. Six Sigma aims to reduce defects and variations to consistently meet customer expectations.

2. Yellow Belts are only responsible for leading large, cross-functional projects.

3. The DMAIC methodology stands for Define, Measure, Analyse, Improve, Control.

4. A SIPOC diagram is used to identify potential causes of defects in a process.

5. In Six Sigma, Yellow Belts often provide guidance to White Belts within their teams.

Section 2: Multiple Choice Questions

6. Which of the following is a primary responsibility of a Yellow Belt?

   o A) Overseeing organisation-wide Six Sigma initiatives

- B) Gathering data and supporting higher-level belts
- C) Developing the project charter for large projects
- D) Conducting advanced statistical analyses for project teams

7. The Measure phase in DMAIC primarily involves:

- A) Establishing goals and objectives for the project
- B) Gathering data to understand the current state of a process
- C) Implementing solutions to address the root causes
- D) Evaluating the feasibility of different improvement ideas

8. A Fishbone Diagram is used to:

- A) Monitor process performance over time
- B) Categorise potential causes of a problem
- C) Set up a data collection plan
- D) Develop a project timeline

9. Which tool helps Yellow Belts assess whether a process can meet customer specifications consistently?

- A) Control Chart
- B) Check Sheet

- C) Process Capability Analysis
- D) Histogram

10. In Six Sigma, the primary purpose of a Control Plan in the Control phase is to:

- A) Outline project goals and objectives
- B) Track and sustain improvements over time
- C) Identify customer requirements for a process
- D) Conduct root cause analysis

Section 3: Short Answer Questions

11. Explain the purpose of a SIPOC diagram in the Define phase.

12. Describe the main role of a Yellow Belt in supporting higher-level belts.

13. What is the main goal of the Improve phase in DMAIC?

14. Define "continuous improvement" in the context of Six Sigma.

15. Why is it important for Yellow Belts to establish a baseline in the Measure phase?

Section 4: Scenario-Based Questions

16. Scenario: A Yellow Belt is asked to reduce response times in customer service. What steps should they take in the Define phase to begin this project?

17. Scenario: During a project, a Yellow Belt identifies high variation in product quality. What tools could they use in the Analyse phase to identify potential causes?

18. Scenario: A Yellow Belt proposes a new procedure to improve accuracy in data entry. How should they test and implement this improvement?

19. Scenario: After implementing a new process in inventory management, the Yellow Belt wants to ensure the changes are maintained. What steps would they take in the Control phase?

20. Scenario: A Yellow Belt is supporting a Green Belt on a cross-departmental project. Describe one way the Yellow Belt can assist with data collection and reporting.

6 Sigma Yellow Belt Answer Sheet

Section 1: True/False Answers

1. True – Six Sigma aims to reduce defects and variations to consistently meet customer expectations.

2. False – Yellow Belts are responsible for leading small, department-focused projects, not large, cross-functional ones.

3. True – DMAIC stands for Define, Measure, Analyse, Improve, Control.

4. False – A SIPOC diagram provides a high-level view of the process, not a list of causes.

5. True – Yellow Belts often guide and mentor White Belts within their teams.

Section 2: Multiple Choice Answers

6. B) Gathering data and supporting higher-level belts – Yellow Belts play a crucial role in data collection and assisting Green and Black Belts.

7. B) Gathering data to understand the current state of a process – The Measure phase is focused on understanding the baseline performance.

8. B) Categorise potential causes of a problem – Fishbone Diagrams help break down and categorise possible causes for analysis.

9. C) Process Capability Analysis – This tool helps determine if a process can consistently meet customer specifications.

10. B) Track and sustain improvements over time – Control Plans ensure that process improvements are maintained and deviations are detected.

Section 3: Short Answer Answers

11. Answer: A SIPOC diagram provides a high-level overview of a process, mapping out Suppliers, Inputs, Process, Outputs, and Customers. It helps define the process boundaries and ensures alignment with customer requirements.

12. Answer: A Yellow Belt's main role in supporting higher-level belts is to gather data, perform initial analysis, assist with implementation, and report on the effectiveness of process changes.

13. Answer: The main goal of the Improve phase is to develop and implement solutions that address the root causes identified in the Analyse phase, improving process performance.

14. Answer: Continuous improvement in Six Sigma refers to an ongoing effort to enhance processes by making incremental improvements, which leads to increased quality, efficiency, and reduced waste.

15. Answer: Establishing a baseline is crucial for measuring improvement. Without a baseline, it's difficult to quantify the impact of changes and determine if the solutions achieve the desired results.

Section 4: Scenario-Based Answers

16. Answer:

- Define the problem by developing a problem statement (e.g., "reduce customer service response times").
- Set clear objectives, such as reducing average response time by a specific amount.
- Identify key stakeholders, like customer service staff and managers, who will support or be affected by the project.

17. Answer:

- Use a Fishbone Diagram to brainstorm potential causes of variation.

- Conduct a Root Cause Analysis using the 5 Whys to explore underlying causes.
- Consider Process Mapping to understand where inefficiencies or variations may occur.

18. Answer:

- Conduct a pilot test of the new procedure on a small scale to measure its impact.
- Gather data on accuracy rates before and after implementation to evaluate effectiveness.
- If successful, develop an implementation plan to roll out the new procedure fully.

19. Answer:

- Develop a Control Plan outlining how to monitor the improved process over time.
- Use a Control Chart to track key metrics and detect any deviations.
- Document the new procedures in SOPs and provide training as needed to sustain improvements.

20. Answer:

- The Yellow Belt can assist by organising and collecting relevant data, such as recording cycle times or error rates.
- They can summarise the data in reports or charts, making it easier for the Green Belt to identify trends and assess performance.

www.ingramcontent.com/pod-product-compliance
Lightning Source LLC
Chambersburg PA
CBHW070107230526
45472CB00004B/1156